Praise for the
POETRY OF SIMON PERCHIK

"... They have a hypnotic quality and the lack of titles draws you restlessly as images form and are taken away to be replaced by juxtaposition or complexity. Perchik uses words to create a world vision uniquely his own."—*New Hope International*

"This is certainly no derivative collection, but rather a unique meditation on the orogeny of a soul."—*Boston Review*

"What is always clear... is that this is a complex, lyrical vision of the commonplace. Even a meager narrative is hardly worth noticing, finally, in the midst of these exquisite imaginings. It is the constant struggle in this process which empowers his poetry and provides tension to his lyric."—*Mid-American Review*

"Some physiologists have claimed that the brain is constructed hologrammatically. A particular memory does not reside in one particular part of the brain, but rather is retained everywhere, and subsequently one part of the brain repeats the whole. Something of this kind of structure has been created by Perchik in this volume."
—*Newsart*

"... Extraordinary linguistic dynamos, a fertile fusion of contrary energies often culminating in masterful performances."—*Poet Lore*

"...Working close to the deeper sources of poetry, in modes reflecting individuality and technical determination, Mr. Perchik is the most original..." —*Poetry*

"So much of what Perchik does include (but leaves at the heart level) is this important thing and I always hear it, as he knows, in what he does." —Charles Olson

"These are poems with fresh insights sticking out all over them and they ought to give pleasure to anyone whose mind is still open to new poetry." —X.J. Kennedy

"... In your poetry words and images appear like sharp fragments of glass, sometimes but not always, smooth rounded by the wash of words coming at us in waves... Reading your poetry, I get a sense of being thrown into a concrete mixer and tumbled with words, and then when stepping beyond the poetry, there is a giddy sense of wobbling without the compass of linearity. And yet, there is a kind of purity in the poems. With some of the poems, I feel like I've stumbled onto a once great city which exists now in ruins..." —James R.Elkins, 29 Legal Studies Forum, 2005

"This is a 'must have' collection of poems penned by one of the greatest living poets writing in the English language. Perchik is a master in combining density, abstraction and powerful imagery, taking the reader to places deep within the unconscious, and exposing that reader to revelations and truths most often fully appreciated only after each poem has been read and given time to be absorbed. That is not to say, however, that the reader will not be deeply impacted while reading the poem—such is the skill with which Perchik leads the reader through his unique emotional labyrinth. The grist for his poetic mill—life, death, love, the natural world—while found in probably all poetry of any worth, is nonetheless treated by Perchik in a cascade of raw emotion and eeriness which makes the reader's journey through his poetry truly special." —Paolo Paravicini

**THE
OSIRIS
POEMS**

THE OSIRIS POEMS

1993–2016

Simon Perchik

Copyright 2017 by Simon Perchik

All rights reserved. No part of this book may be reproduced in any form or by any means without permission from the publisher.

Published by boxofchalk
www.forgejournal.com

Names: Perchik, Simon, author.
Title: Osiris Poems, 1993–2016 / Simon Perchik.
Description: Lincoln: boxofchalk, 2017.
ISBN—13: 978-0-6926-2883-6 (paperback).
BISAC: POETRY / American / General.

Set in Minion Pro

ABOUT THE AUTHOR

Simon Perchik, an attorney, was born 1923 in Paterson, NJ and educated at New York University (BA English, LLB Law). His poems have also appeared in various literary journals including *Partisan Review, Poetry, The Nation* and *The New Yorker.*

Other works by
SIMON PERCHIK

THE ELIZABETH PRESS:
I Counted Only April (1964); *Twenty Years of Hands* (1966); *Which Hand Holds the Brother* (1969); *Hands You Are Secretly Wearing* (1972); *Both Hands Screaming* (1975); and *The Club Fits Either Hand* (1979).

LINWOOD PUBLISHERS:
The Snowcat Poems — To the Photographs of Robert Frank (1984).

SHEARSMAN BOOKS:
Mr Lucky (1984); *Shearsman 19* (1994).

THE SCARECROW PRESS:
Who Can Touch These Knots, New & Selected Poems (1985).

WHITE PINE PRESS:
The Gandolf Poems (1987).

FLOCKOPHOBIC PRESS:
Birthmark (1992).

DUSTY DOG PRESS:
Redeeming the Wings (1991); *The Emptiness between My Hands* (1993); *These Hands Filled with Numbness* (1996).

ST. ANDREWS COLLEGE PRESS:
Letters to the Dead (1993).

PAVEMENT SAW PRESS:
Hands Collected (2000). (A reprinting of the above 16 books); 2nd ed. (2003).

STRIDE PUBLICATIONS:
Touching the Headstone (2000).

SPLIT/SHIFT:
The Autochthon Poems (2001)

RIVER OTTER PRESS:
Almost Rain (2013)

POETS WEAR PRADA
The B Poems (2016)

REPOSITORIES

Library of Congress, The Rare Book Collection

Yale University Library, The Beinecke Rare Book & Manuscript Collection

Ohio State University Library, Avant Writing Collection

For Andrea Moorhead
Editor of Osiris *where all the poems
in this collection appeared, some in
earlier versions.*

*I further acknowledge my debt to
James L. Weil, Edward Butscher
and Anselm Parlatore for their poetry
and friendship; to Deborah Light for
the generous access to her voluminous
collection of myths; to the owners,
employees and customers of both Fierro's
Pizzeria and The Golden Pear
where these poems were written.*

CONTENTS

What you hear could be a mountain   1
It takes more flickering, wires   2
The Earth dazed from thirst   3
As a narrow breeze   4
Even the sun is terrified   6
Face up this darkness   8
All night a loneliness :one seed   10
Still in a trance, this photograph   11
A stain that never heals —at the wound   12
As if my lips have learned to weep   13
This granite has sea in it, each splash   14
These wings I smooth :a dim light   15
I too had swallowed a star :a cry   16
This watch already gathering   17
Even across a table   18
It must recognize these trees, this rain   19
With such a downward stroke   20
You tried to say, Send distances   21
There's a fragrance to light   22
From nowhere, a star overflows   23
And I lean   24
And the sun in ashes   25
Stone, stone, stone, not a drop   26

Now that the planes are gone   27
Then nudging the cold engine block   28
And the sun too, goes south   30
This time the splinter, wedged   31
These iron faucets, one   32
And the headwind still visible   34
Even without their feathers, kisses   35
To start the limp you lace   36
This handle slopes the way each fountain   38
Each night these branches lift off   39
You try to make sense, the radiator   40
This twig needs leaves, its bark   42
Even this envelope carries in its breath   43
Lifted too close this leaf   44
This shallow dish dead center   45
You climb and these steps spread out   46
It takes both faucets and each night   47
Attack and this hillside   48
It must welcome this light   50
Between each breast a darkness   51
You can tell by the curtain   52
You constantly need watering   54
You limp and her casket   56
To protect itself this pond   57
But where is the river   58
As if the sun lets its darkness   59
This scaled down backhoe, kept yellow   60
Between two fingers the dirt   61

This twig could just as easily   62
And this stone turns its back   63
This newspaper and each evening   64
And though they're cold   65
Together with your knees   66
As if this dirt can't overflow   67
To coax this rake you dig   68
All that's left from the map   69
You can tell by the heat   70
You reach into that darkness   71
This branch climbs past you   72
You stack dried newspaper   73
At the end this sand coming by   74
Once it reaches this sink   75
Not yet certain, half stone   76
By the handful, in tenderness   77
Another fold though the paper   78
With roots that glow in the dark   79
Star by star you add a word   80
This stone on your forehead   81
Even if these waves are calmed   82
With a sudden glow one leg   83
Windswept, this radio   84
As if a rope, half bone   85
This battered window box   86
You were buried in the afternoon   87
It was a needless rinse, this bowl   88
It's not a map yet there's hope   89

It's what you do, the mirror 90
You learn to hammer in the dark 91
As if these gravestones were once a forest 92
What was siphoned off the sun 93
And stubborn yet these wicks 94
You never get used to it 95
When you come, come singing 96
What's left is its wingtip 97
You draw a star on the calendar 98
What did you expect! with just its scent 99
You weakened the paint with salt 100
You walk clinging to streams 101
Everything on this wall clouds over 102
Plane after plane till all the pieces 103
Drop by drop, its silence 104
Side by side a planet that has no star 105
The rock that sparked a supernova 106
A few hours and all the stars 107
You fill in the name then prop it 108
Although you wait for midnight 109

To Mickie

THE
OSIRIS
POEMS

*

What you hear could be a mountain
—this is more than just a toy, it's bent
the way every arch sucks up the ground
makes a fountain from trees and galaxies
—take it! use both hands

in case there's a wing
or the light that never closes
leaves a space where the darkness between
pulls your arms overhead
—what you hear

could be grass, it's hard to guess
but the silence must come
from what once was nothing but sunlight
was only a feathery whisper
taking so long, and this flower
even you have forgotten.

*

It takes more flickering, wires
tied the way a harp is held
and my wrist further till it turns
between two suns at once

—they don't last long, one
already night, tired
though my fingers still give it milk
and lullabies —one

throwing away its light
as if my arm would rest for awhile
and on this table with dishes
set for flowers, skies side to side

—I can't hold on, my hands
half lightning, half this bulb
already twinkle, twinkle, little
singing and the dark.

*

The Earth dazed from thirst
and streams not yet pouring
—ice, thin and weakened, drips, first
hammers off the smaller stones
to rebuild the pitcher and the slope

—the water will plunge, each Spring
and under my footsteps
again the reeking mud :you will drink
till every creek and my shadow
opens its torn umbrella :the sun
over my shoulder, haggard.

I bring you a flower
as even the seas dive into rock
for water —this bloom
will bleach slowly, like a train
with only one passenger no one sees.

Only you. And the shovelfuls
and when does this ice
weightless all winter, knocking
as if there was still a cup
and you had a tablecloth, expecting me.

*

As a narrow breeze
peeled from some stone
every night a comet
wandering its rind and pits :an orchard
thinner and thinner
trailing itself, circling itself
sliced like the skin from an apple
soaking in water —each night

as if this stone in my hand
was made from your shadow
and your eyes like twins
coming from nowhere to open my hand
to get a better look
to lift the edge.

It's night
as kids will duck for fruit :the sun
swallowed with some sky
that tasted like water

and this stone no one sees anymore
holds down your shadow
and mine —nothing moves
except a stone
carried one shadow to another

scattering its dust
to rebuild the world, the hearts
Gemini once carried
and every night I call your name
twice, breathe into your name
as if a door would open
and a house appear, you

can't breathe out and the night
cuts everything in half, this breeze
never again two by two :each raindrop
alone, gusting under the ground
under my arms still carrying
this stone and doll-like evenings.

*

Even the sun is terrified
hiding from stars :kisses
that refire the moon
—you will think it's morning
this time for good, the moonlit breeze
lifting its great shadow
as in that story where a boy
and his carpet or words
windblown on some yellowing, torn page

—you will squint, your heart
carry the blizzard under each breath
under you lips
—you will think you're flying
pulling from your lips
handfuls where weeds
crack open steep cliffs
to refill the lightning bolt in your back
—you'll think it's air

breathe in these stars
let the sun come back
only to rest, some shade
not too high, behind the yard
and trees unraveling to snow.

You will bandage the sun
with your shadow
lift its darkness too weak now
to even lean under your shoulder

—you kiss! higher, so high these stars
as a snowdrift stamping its feet
that once were yours
and stone. And dancing.

And from all that light
you spill out a knife
and the sun which never took root
lies still for the wound
refills the sky, the kiss
the kiss, the kiss, the kiss, the kiss and kiss.

*

Face up this darkness
almost catching fire, the wallpaper
side by side like a door closing
clicks! the old bulb brooding again
exploded, tried to dry its heart
as every night soaks up
the still dripping Earth
—this cremated bulb
started out red :a shade
calling everyone home
more and more trains
till no light made it through
and the mouths one on top another
so black even stars can't get out

—you pour more coffee
afraid my fingers are too dry, pour
till the air is without air
is an endless grate :a fountain
rubbing its sleeve on a list
read outloud to those eyes
that sound like words
and you make believe it's words.

That damn train again! Pouring
as if a train was passing
and its rails dripping —Here Here Here
Here :names on every wall, Here Here
on the ledges, Here Here Here on the margins
Here on the question marks! their names
must grow inside those trees
huddled then cooked into paper —no name
rises out, no name wipes off
or these packed walls
enroute to the stacks, the riverbanks
the smallest branches stopped listening

—you pour the cracked cup for yourself
know it's the one I will grab
like the light from another room :a boxcar
creaking, filled with shadows
holding on to a wall
as if they could stop
or this bulb dark enough
black enough, ever in time.

*

All night a loneliness :one seed
and the rain not yet harvested
is allowed to dry —by morning
the color which gives each drop its name

—in this low sky the caves
the damp campfires where rain is shared
and each child learns to wish

—without a leaf or fruit
a milk-white sprout
scraping at my stove
as if the twigs inside
felt the wind again

—all night a dim fire
staring at its rust
at the mist melted into memory

—through such a wedge
even the sun has lost its way
cries out and no morning
to move closer. Or stars.

*

Still in a trance, this photograph
—I have to lift your arms
pulled motionless from the paper

midair :an old dance
trains me to fly
and the sky whose cold can't fall

or begin another year
—there's no room for arms
for the wide victory roll

claiming the air, forming the lake
fixed in ice miles above
—I have to point, grip my breath

and pull —I could claw but not yourself
—this picture whose only cry
is the cloud, the call me, call me.

*

A stain that never heals —at the wound
this bowl taking on water, dead flowers
—I lean —my lips so close

is already a flower
split down the middle
—with the same warm water

softly toward the water that can't leave
—behind this great stone my back
bending more when the sun is full

rolled tight —it's natural your grave
should be round, talking
always about a journey

or dragging back another stone
each night heavier and stars
are growing on the sun —maybe it is Spring.

Maybe this sky, fading, yellow, weakened
side to side so close
leans on your hand and the melting.

*

As if my lips have learned to weep
—after all these years
the evenings need more room

—my mouth is used to darkness
and goodbyes, kisses, though my eyes
were closed and now this spit trickles

place to place, covered with feathers
—it does no good, these sleeves
are soaked, held closer

than lifting your arms
and all that time your arms
filling with mist and your arms

seep through my lips —a great wave
unable to hold back
the hidden sea and your stillness.

*

This granite has sea in it, each splash
a bell —water lets nothing forget
and drop by drop even stone goes mad

carves by a small saucer for tears
for the tormented miles away
ringing out —I come to scream

to become a bowl and the white smoke
rising where your lips still drift
under the pounding snow —this stone

has tides in it, smells from rainfall
and decay and your arms too are in my throat
in the distance, in the tightening.

*

These wings I smooth :a dim light
lifts off, my jacket
hanging on to rotted sky and haze

and the attic still climbs
banks into the storm —mice
must love to fly —my wings

painted blue so long ago
and somehow a cloud among this mess
—it's cold up here

—box to box, the planes
unpack, starting up
—what the mice hear is the wait

to trap the sun :the polish
gives so much away
and now the sky

—what they hear is rain
is the mad kept alive
by breathing through their heart

—they hear the wind
shaped by this furious rag
kept empty, smelling from names.

*

I too had swallowed a star :a cry
seen only at night and this small room
sits by its window

—you can hear the wall
holding back the light almost till morning
—in time your hand loses interest
opens, aches to be left alone

and the star you know is there
—it's been so long, it must be shabby
—offer it something, slowly
and not lose the way —in my jaws

one cry stays fixed —no other star
is guided by the dead
kept from falling too fast
and in my breathing where you belong.

*

This watch already gathering
—who would imagine winter
and you are holding my wrist
listening as if the way back
would lift my arm —snow too
is sorted into stones
and not stones, into eyes
that never move —do you still have lips?

This window too will close —every gesture
resets, veers into the Earth
into a morning and the Earth
still struggling to stay aloft
—even light is collecting, some darkness
here, there, here

and the watch each day slower
—what you hear is calling for you, is the dirt
gone lame, wary, step by step
dragging a place, encrusted, lost
and the frost between two stones
held fast to accept the cold
and among your eyes.

*

Even across a table
the separated miles
—everything I touch becomes dark
becomes stars
and struggling through the Earth
in time for evening.

I can hear the names
—they never give up
and through this table
is moving closer

—I don't answer the dead
but my eyes ache from gusts
homeward into a withered tree
a falling in the dark
and under my arms
the light almost green, almost here.

*

It must recognize these trees, this rain
coming back —it never forgot
the migration routes :each cloud

still with a trace when the sun
no day, no night, only green
that in these leaves even now

reminds the rain what time once was
—in such a mist these raindrops
not yet sealed

not yet filled with the constant search
for ground —even today a stone
will run from the sky, hug roots

not the branches and this rain
as a gesture, lets you fold your arms
over it —you feel its light

working loose to leave your heart
and each breath underwater
coming back for stray bottom sand

for the lost sun and even you
are tears, wander off into days, into nights
and these warm leaves the last.

*

With such a downward stroke
judgments are sealed and the child
bent over this blackboard

will soon finish the numeral 1
stroke the damp fur :the chalk
stretching its neck —on this darkness

the Great Bear will feed forever
edging toward the galaxies
—nothing is wasted, even now

at one end this thin line
the light starts out —from the other
step by step the dead

toward the middle and my hand too
is at home on the night sky
is counting each finger

with a beginner's 1
and in the center a sudden cup
a hollow palm where the dim light

loses its way from one cry
then another
and the emptiness between my hands.

*

You tried to say, Send distances
missing all these years —words
don't need a mouth
for a landmark —they find their way
through stones in riverbeds
in old bread that has your soft voice
your drifting away, hands closed.

It's not a particular bird
that the bath in the backyard
thaws and the water in your lips
becomes dark red :a great wave
come back from somewhere far
sweeping away and in my arms

—I send you distances —one by one
one from this bird, one from
these few seeds
and I am over the world
feeding the world through Spring
through its Winter.

You tried to say and this birdbath
whose stones still damp from the beach
huddle —I drink from here
as in a small cemetery
after a warm rainfall and my mouth
fills with flowers and distances.

*

There's a fragrance to light
—it won't let you forget
filling with ashes and loneliness

—it's now more difficult to breathe
somewhere that wants to be forgotten
as a dark cry that belonged to the sun
—it broods a full 24 hours
and its scent holding fast
makes a crust :this light

knew it would be made from wood
would burn even its first cry
kept near your heart growing to fit
the day that's longer than all the others

—the light becomes too heavy, stays damp
though no one is weeping in your arms
—you breathe in the way this mountain
is holding you and on the way home.

*

From nowhere, a star overflows
pouring its light across your lips
and some old love song

—who can remember every word
—even the sun by evening
leaves empty :you learn to forget

so the melody will flicker off
fall apart in your mouth
—a few lines, that's it!

What a shame, such a voice
but you can't remember
complain the lamps are arranged

too far apart, too dim
then move room to room
with the words that are left

are exhausted, sweating and glowing
—the roof and the moon are both flying
filled with a huge chorus

and the clear light across the world
—you forget —without looking
a song half lost, half through the rafters.

*

And I lean
the way the moon breathes out
looks for the hidden slope
that began at the dunes —the waves
losing their foothold, never heard again.

I bend over this iron pail
to empty out my silence
in bits, no longer that clear blue
and the sky who quiets even stone
weighs more than my floor.

This is my sea! twisted in place
by a mop, by a loading
and unloading, used to coming back
between the rock sharp walls :a coast
that almost hears my voice taking root
under the white cliffs
and from out its shadow a lily
every Spring to look for something
it's never seen.

You will arrive by sea
not call at all but in one box
opened after another and my hands
helplessly spinning in foam
where your lips have begun to shine
already with beach grass, lotions and salt.

*

And the sun in ashes
leaning against this mist
not yet split into logs

—you once flew through the sun
without its flames, went blind
watching how its light peels off
half born, half glowing in your stove
half no smoke yet, whose shadow
still has some heat left

is older than the ground
and every morning held down
by rope, never loose again

—even without your eyes
the vapor trails still pull the sun
closer to its fire, to this iron gate
left out in the cold the way a net
is carried across a desert, sifts
for missing branches, birds
the light covered over, still breathing.

*

Stone, stone, stone, not a drop
some watermark that witnessed
here was once a sea —all that's left
is stone, still obsessed
floats out, falling back twice every day
in the same place —you can't leave.

You on one side and my shoulders
bent under the stone so you
could follow it out forever
cover the Earth with waves
that have no sound —even the rivers

are stone, their banks warning stones
as if your name would have no meaning
when read aloud and love
is such a blessing
with nothing but stone between us

—you on one side can't see how my skin
torn off, my knuckles lock in place
writing on soft paper, over and over
and over and over though your name
has just two words
used to the bandages, scars, silences.

*

Now that the planes are gone
the air weighs almost nothing
left out to die and rivers
still trying to dodge, stalked
there and back —on this roadmap
an invisible string curls into flames
circles down, looking for bridges
and just above the horizon
what once was a moon
loses its home in the fire

—the sky from so far off
pouring through me bone by bone
looking for the deep breath that waits
on every map though they don't show
the rain, just the distances
—they like names, name everywhere
but skies —they work the folds

so I never forget how huge
how easily and my arms
climbing toward cities on paper
with wings, with the scent
from streets burnt to the ground.

*

Then nudging the cold engine block
he picks an apple, pleased
with its color, with leaning
on a branch where his elbow
feels the small fire, then waits

for the lingering and almost daybreak
whose shadow would hold up the sun
half wax, half wing, half
the hood resting on one shoulder
—what did he lose under this visor

under the iron breastplate
the tower no longer on horseback
and the slow oil leak that carves
one drop from another

—every bolt already clamped
the way stalactites, stone by grieving stone
—every drop falling motionless
strikes another as rain once formed mountains
and trembling creeks still helpless
on the ground —he picks a wrench

by its size as if it had ripened
deep inside some cave where rain
had never stopped and he leans
half spilling over the dark wall
half tightening its endless water.

*

And the sun too, goes south
—in back its cave
it could outlast the winter

though I grind this axe
from behind, the stone
turned over and over

for rivers hid under
slowed down, flickering
with gills and those pinecones

who still have their scales
hang around for showers
—I name this grindstone

Angel Falls and between two fingers
the needle thin afternoon
stays green, filled with bees

with honey, berries
and the smoke sweetening
—I name every tree

so what I say is like yours
a good name, that's warmed
from further and further away.

*

This time the splinter, wedged
the way even a board fights back
—warpaint! your thumb tipped

with peroxide and just above the ridge
falling birds, falling branches, your finger
already infected, changing colors

is swollen with rivers as if one arm
weighs more and slowly the poison
sifts for dirt, soaks in

beginning to sting where your finger
caresses a hinge, a lid, a kiss
and this needle-thin paint

a deadly brown, a suddenness
that takes down even moonlight
once it touches the skin and dries.

*

These iron faucets, one
for water from the South, its twin
icy streams and every morning
I turn two valves
the way each child is born
from riverbeds and the sink

filling with skies, with open seas
where the sun looks at its reflection
—the light half wind
half bathing the Earth

—every morning a few drops
on my forehead, just enough sunlight
to remind us all how death
when this bowl drains
as if a great wave, beginning at sunrise
continent over continent —you see it

in stands when the crowds
wait for the crest to be carried
together, washing the water
with water not yet whirlpools and absences

—I hold these two tools
not sure what it is I'm making
or loosening or stone
from stones that weep
even in wells, were brought to this basin
and like a sudden flower
points where the sun and my hand too
wants to go home.

*

And the headwind still visible
charred the way you use both hands
to steady this grill, bank its grate

into some battered, climbing turn
as if this fire could untangle
replace the sky with another sky

while your eyes burn to the ground
—your breath nurses the smoke higher
smells from rust and engine oil

and one arm under your heart, the other
rebuilt with gristle and bone and glue :ashes
used over and over for screaming.

*

Even without their feathers, kisses
all that's left though your lips
somehow remember the sunlit ravines, open
the way mourners still warm their hands
single file, let the silence
carry them up, who know
where in the ground each breath
is heated, lifted and your throat made soft

—whispers are what you want, you listen
for the returning stones, for clouds, agree
to distances —you wait for mist
still damp from some lifeless sea
weightless below its eyes
that can barely see the rain
—you open your lips and the drizzle
has this echo, drink
from a sky carved from stone
a small stone who loves you.

*

To start the limp you lace
the way all mothers remember
and the warm, dark rivergrass
where birds still nest

—you tie one shoe tighter
till its shell cracks open
and under each fingernail the pieces
smell from damp mud, broken reeds
riverside —the bow stays wet

as if each egg learned long ago
to cling without flying away
—with each step feathers everywhere
dragged while the other shoe

is washed in bronze, carries you off
for later —you squeeze one foot
so the other will harden, grow
wingtips for its powerful dive

towards stone and you walk forever
high up on your toes, spreading out
the limp all shells hear breaking apart
crumbling into footsteps

and shoreline, creaking
as if some cradle would suddenly
be heard in the birds all night
who sing to it, followed slowly
by mountainsides and drought.

*

This handle slopes the way each fountain
still remembers it was once a sun
a great arm towering and over the Earth
its shadow becomes too heavy
oozes along the ground —you pump

just for the darkness
carry it up by the mouthfuls
by the stones that can't move anymore
or change color or open

to attract the morning
before it touches the dirt
or harden —you drink with your shoulders
almost in flames, almost
holding back the sun
and over the cup your fingers
tighten into the slow, wide turn
that no longer climbs by itself —one arm
heavier, filled with heartbeats
and the emptiness alongside.

*

Each night these branches lift off
dragging a tree
that is not a scarecrow

and though your jacket is unbuttoned
it flaps in the wind
to attract those birds

who believe leaves can migrate
once they learn more colors
—you invite the flutter

into these wide lapels
that need more feathers
for their descent, for the wings

each flock knows you grow
inside your sleeves
from water and darkness

—on both sides the sun's the same
just month after month
half thirst, half nightfalls

that aren't afraid anymore
when your shadow leans over the Earth
and drinks with its tiny eyelids open.

*

You try to make sense, the radiator
won't cool though its slender hose
is already covered with winter

layer on layer —you guess
it's the windshield, every breeze
overheats and under the tinted glass

the smoke rises a dark blue
—for a split second the sky holds
to the surface and from this distance

some priest measures the ram
led over the greasy pit
where the mechanic snaps a cold tool

on ancient rivers and your throat.
It snows with new parts, your lips
almost human, almost one finger

pressed against the still sharp key
—it shakes with a climb
that is not a bird, not the sun

or the scent from a graceful turn
about to say something

slowly barely flesh
—it starts when the hood
closes though no one
is inside or weeping.

*

This twig needs leaves, its bark
half snow, half mountainside
but what brought you?

Don't be fooled by its icy glaze
crouched over your gravestone
as if the prowling sun
would devour it on the way
to your lips that are not mornings

—by now you should be used to twigs
trying to warm you, make a nest
and the Earth little by little so tiny
a sky has begun to circle my fingertip

—a simple touch from overhead
and even a stone comes to life
cries out from hunger
as if my mouth is filled
with kisses, with roots and birdsong.

*

Even this envelope carries in its breath
the breeze from distant wings, planes
hidden the way birds change color
and with each sunset gather in

though the runway is overgrown, is feeble
has become your fingers :flaps raised
as if the sky inside
needs more altitude and slowly

lifting you over an old airfield
that has fallen across the Earth
as a shadow torn apart, half paper, half
roadway and the truck from the Post Office

makes the run to some city
and back, midair, tighter and tighter
till every letter breaks into pieces
into chaff, into rain and headwind.

*

Lifted too close this leaf
fastens on your sleeve and dries
—it must know why one ear
hears sooner than the other
forces you to turn and climb
till there's nothing left
to lose, the sun
worthless, the air
limping, poisonous

—you hold in your arm
what every tree finds too heavy
throws out and even in winter
you pick up from there
crumple your fingers till their bones
want to live at the bottom
but only one recognizes oak
from when the moon fills up the sea
drop by drop and your knuckles
pounding against each other.

*

This shallow dish dead center
though its glass is commonplace
shimmering into mist

—it's not the usual birth
or that fragrance still moist
from the womb, reaching out

to be born in the open
—you cool this tea
the way every breath

divides in half then half again
and again till all that's left
is snow —what you drink

already has your eyes, your lips
and between your hands
its scent ices over where once

there was nothing —side to side
you darken this water as if the moon
still rocks the Earth asleep

—you sip this darkness
let it stain your voice
your whispers frozen to the bottom.

*

You climb and these steps spread out
in those rings trees still carry
under their wings

—you collect height
and at night two at a time
though the steps are chipped
the inscriptions worn away
staring off to the side

—they will be first
spruced back to life
and at the top you move the sun back
—crosswinds can't be trusted
always on the run, raging inside
close to your throat

—you carry up the dust
the Earth turned away, step by step
this wall all there is to lead you safely
against her eyes already hollowed out
as if in all this stone
there's no place to lie down
no room for your hand
that suddenly will open
and over your lips the stars
breathing down, count for nothing.

*

It takes both faucets and each night
you fill the sink the way mourners
set up camp —one alongside the other

swaying and your legs half open
wait till it's dark, kneel down
as if it was not your own

and it's safe to drink from the rim
beside the zebras. the leopards
—this lake won't freeze or dig up

your footprints from the falling snow
calling for help and in the cold
you wipe your lips on the wall.

*

Attack and this hillside
shows its teeth :each stone
drips with saliva

and even the glaze
can't tell the difference
— you dig till the sun

enters at last
staggering the way each evening
is burned to the ground

laid bare in the smoke
all stones smell when struck
one against the other

and the dirt dragged away
still struggling
—you only want to share

though your hands won't dry
and each year less room
—you dig as if each hole

is filled with shoreline
could be held back

rebuilt from waves
from valleys and mountain streams
that whiten these stones
with cheeks and emptiness.

*

It must welcome this light
sent up, banished and the sun
overflowing still can't wait

till morning —you will open the door
for something you're not sure, make room
the way a tree rests its branches

higher and higher and the room
kept empty for evenings
on their way back, bone-tired

hollowed out, barren, cold
and the door take in
the darkness :the dying down

and the slow, climbing turn
for which there is no word
no sound or below.

*

Between each breast a darkness
clean to the bone —always a shadow
the way all love notes are folded

over and over till all that's left
is the paper the nights are written on
half moonlight, half that black ink

the sun knows by heart :a wound
still fresh, flowing forever
as memory and stars carved out

shredded for one constellation more
that once belonged to the Earth
and always in place —between your breasts

trees grow, shaded paths and the scent
from when a shovel digs another heart
for another tree —you still use those hearts

as if night after night the sky
has not yet grown over
and even in the dark its stars hold on.

*

You can tell by the curtain
how the play will end, this sill
dusted word for word
till your ear slides along
the feathers and you hear
a door open the way
between the passenger's side
and just one wing
so there's a spin in the works
though under the hood
an old campfire is fed
live songs laced together
with stories about ghosts
—their smoke covers you
—even the tires
glistening, half wood
half songs, surrounded
by miles no one remembers
and the invisible shadow
alongside your eyes when the door
opens on the driver's side
divides the sky the way lightening
sees what's coming and the curtain
makes a gesture —spread-eagle
then climbs slowly
to become your arms

—you don't move
—from this height the sky
fills with some moon-lit constellation
still burning in the dark
—you can make out the beak
the claws clasping your lips
suddenly rock, lowered here
to watch over the dead
the falling birds
with not enough air to breathe.

*

You constantly need watering
—from pity and these leaves
thumping the ground your heart

remembers the sound for
though there's no dry twig
to pull apart where the wind

still forks, unaware
it changed direction
to close your eyes

—you are watered by leaves
clinging to the grass
that fell from this same tree

and never dries
—all that happens
is their shadows taking root

heated the way a bird
is sure each egg
has its fire inside, will fly

with the bone in its breast
pulling the Earth apart
while you hold between your hands

a small stone already dead
brought down from a great height
and left to open.

*

You limp and her casket
breaking open, its splinters
lose hold and this dirt

is water again, each ripple
wider and wider drags ashore
though the pebble you tossed

covers the sea with a darkness
that spends its life drowning
—a tiny rock broken off

from your step by step holding on
forever —you walk on water, close
to the crater's rim half wood

half storm, half where her voice
could be mistaken for moonlight
for the one stone more who in the end

is dead and you lift it
gently, lower it to your lips
as if it was a whisper, or a mouth.

*

To protect itself this pond
freezes over, fills with light
the way the first mother on Earth

made it safely ashore
taking her child along
though you are still thirsty

cold, half ice, half comforted
by this ancient flower
blooming now as snow

—this knee-deep pond
once overflowed with power
could insist on Spring

would lean against the sun
till it begins to heat again
taste from salt and open sea

—you can look through
see where the straight line began
and keeps arriving

as if every cradle at night
is rocking in water
and the now invisible silence.

*

But where is the river
—not one inch closer
though the will to win
has outlasted you
the way sunlight slows
loses out to the cold

—there must have been a wound
a rock and that someplace
the dead are waiting for
while you watch how the horizon
slowly ices over, carries you
into open sea where your breath
lies down on the darkness

and drinks from this half the sky
lets the other side take the lead
eating away at these stars
sprawled out as shoreline

—you are surrounded at last
clouded over by moonlight
and nothing but moonlight.

*

As if the sun lets its darkness
take hold and night after night
your hand begin that vague ripple

from there to here —your arm becomes
some ancient wave and you can't stop
or slow the unraveling

or along each step by step
the stillness all light attracts
once it stands at the door

—you have no choice! it's hello
or be left, breathing in
just to stretch out and keep moving

—you can't be born
without these stars in motion
—you can't die either

though each evening brings you
another mourner, one alongside the other
nomads along the road where once

a dark sea covered the sky
set it adrift, first as a warm breeze
then the hillsides slowly over your heart.

*

This scaled down backhoe, kept yellow
the way butterflies suddenly lose interest
though its hard-hat operator

likes the risk, touches down
and between the cemetery rows takes hold
as if once here was farmland

with no sunlight left, just these sites
half under construction, half
your jittery eyelids —you watch

how a crop is harvested stone by stone
and by instinct you sift —not here
not there, then try again inches away

shake your invisible wings in the open
alone, alone, rootless and for a split second
another night begins and ends.

*

Between two fingers the dirt
still greets these dead
coming by with open eyes
then rain that can't hold on

—this strange handshake
over and over warms your arm
though the sun fell short
missing the Earth

the way a hillside stops growing
if no one touches it
as flowers whose colors
can no longer remember

or face this arm
the one you bring too near
chosen for its memory
its power and sound.

*

This twig could just as easily
be a hurricane, drained then swept away
though it must sense downhill

with dying wood —what you collect
you steady between two fingers
already sunlight and ashes

and any second now
this scrap left for dead
will split in half and disbelief

—a random snap
as if you had forgotten
to count backwards, not sure
once you reach the emptiness

it will still answer, tell you
how to follow behind
well after well, filled

with passageways and slowly
you take up the slack, the unfit
the shaky wearing out in a circle

half sunlight, half chasing off
the cold broken open, infected
with fires that never recover.

*

And this stone turns its back
the way streams even in snow
crush you under the descent

smelling from moonlight
and toward each other
though there's still some rain inside

all night flowing beneath your feet
as gravel and whispers
—with one sharp stone

you open your mouth as if she
is more thirsty than the others
and every path glows with ice

is singing that old love song
carried in your arms
clearing the way to her lips

and one by one each night
heavier, reaches up
for the darkness and go.

*

This newspaper and each evening
another gate is raised
spreads across some infield

miles from the game
—you reach for the ball
and without a sound the moon

goes wild in the dark
already rolling off the Earth
and in this still warm glove

the catch you read about
sitting in the stuffed chair
suddenly on its feet

torn open, blown forward
further and further
almost at the stadium

turning you page by page
into shoulders, into distances
into this invisible sunrise

everywhere at once —sleep now
is impossible, the floor too far
too restless even with the lights on.

*

And though they're cold
they won't answer to a single name
from when these flowers

covered the air with stone
and room for your shadow
where nothing was before

—what they want is more darkness
not these graves bunched the way bells
still overturn as that night sky

even you can't wear for an earring
hear this dirt making the emptiness
somewhere inside your arms.

*

Together with your knees
already half hands
—even the sky is lessened

lets this rain speak for two
the way stars leave you
—you come too close

and though you whisper
the dirt collapses, cools
till no one can escape

except their darkness
and the distance
that is not rain, that clings

tightens, makes from your voice
each cry smaller and smaller
back into your arms.

*

As if this dirt can't overflow
has nothing behind it
except your fingertips
further and further apart

—you look for the waterline
the way each morning dries
closing in on you, half crater
half while this clay jar

begins to drink again
with its mouth and the flower
at home with you, here and there
covers you and nothing between.

*

To coax this rake you dig
a nest, your shoulder
already growing feathers

weighs almost nothing
and more than anyplace else
its shadow flutters, lowers

along the branches :the sun
must sense how huge it is
and these leaves everywhere

have begun to carry back
its mornings, making room
as handful by handful

the way each hole circles down
to begin again, fills
with winter then with distances.

*

All that's left from the map
is this birdbath —you can't make out
the north, northeast or if the wind

is in the same place, skimming
lower and lower as shoreline
not sure you're still there

or did the water dry by itself
—you rely on it, need this landmark
to locate exactly where

and you make the sharp turn
deep into birdsong and the cries
that follow behind, end over end

with both hands and the ground
spills out its air, there's room
for you and in all directions.

*

You can tell by the heat
though they long ago gave up
the search for water and air

and with every death another
comes to this dry riverbed
already hillside, warmed

by some invisible spore
deep inside and your hands
around it, closed

the way each footpath slows
still gathering the others
who take too long in the curve

—all these rocks! and the dirt
peels off till what you hear
is everywhere the sun

not yet born and in your arms
bit by bit broken apart
with care and mornings.

*

You reach into that darkness
stars return for, are cooled
and yet you open the mail

slowly so in each envelope
the letter folding over and over
still falls out as mist

covers the ground
almost to a boil —you retrace
the way the blind find shelter

and with just your fingertips
empty the small fire
hidden behind the others

waiting for its shadow
cut off from home
and at the slightest touch.

*

This branch climbs past you
the way a breeze spreads out
warmed by roots and feathers

—that's why when you look down
the fruit changes its colors
sweetened with leaves and eyes

that are all alike though the tree
no longer feeds on slower trees
or regrets the choice it made

—its wood still rises, is sure
water will come and wings
still possible, not yet too heavy

from after so much death
so much dirt to shade
and already underway.

*

You stack dried newspaper
the way every tower keeps track
where the others are —in every room

as if this clutter could darken
would guide you into the open
growing over the usual rain

and stars impossible to find alone
—this tiny apartment is held down
though the ceiling is kept invisible

in place on these maps you need
for all Norths to begin as pillars
and the way back.

*

At the end this sand coming by
covers you with soft flowers
that long ago dried as footsteps

still treading inside some shallow grave
smothered as afterward and dust
—you loved her the way the Earth

keeps warm and between two suns
place to place what's left
you walk without looking down

though your arms are closing
have grown together a single fingertip
touching these shells and pebbles.

*

Once it reaches this sink
the sun takes nothing back
lets you place water

and forever it's your shadow
wandering the Earth
the way all twins are born

already cold —you rinse
as if moonlight were leaving it
damaged, a scar would come

so this cup you hold you hold
twice, gropes alongside
as darkness though the faucet

still leaks, flows through your arms
draining hillside after hillside
from riverbeds and almost there.

*

Not yet certain, half stone
half held back —wave after wave
rattles it, makes it start over

louder, distracted by the sound
that is not your shoulders
gathering around this grave

no longer facing the fragrance
riverbeds become once they dry
by calling out to each other

clog your mouth with salt and nearby
—what you hear is edging closer
has doubts, lost count

the way these rocks are winded
and one by one broken up
as flowers and your arms.

*

By the handful, in tenderness
yet your shadow erupts
and by nightfall holds on

one shoulder then the other
spun as if this dirt would find
the wind it came here for

circle up and cover this place
with your finger touching
the grave skies grow into

and never let go —a parting gesture
collecting darkness with another
helps you leave the way the dead

fill their arms with the Earth
carried around as morning and higher
in stones they know by heart.

*

Another fold though the paper
is already clogged, scented
with granite —this endless letter

lies down exhausted, spaces
appear over and over
then emptied by hand

—it happens every time, the ink
dries without lips, no mouth
nothing between this page

and the hour after hour
where every word is her name
wants it down in black and white

left in the open the way you learned
to speak through stone, whisper
as if you were still living.

*

With roots that glow in the dark
you approach each grave
the way all wood remembers

its first wish was moonlight
and overwhelmed the Earth
as mornings that grow only in dirt

—you lean across, breathing in
breathing out to exchange places
though the ground is decorated

with nothing more than itself
stubborn, still filled for campfires
and all around are the beads

outlined in the shadows, woven
slowly row by row, fondled
and endless songs about travelers.

*

Star by star you add a word
the way the Earth still darkens
from the bottom up, lets you hold on

keep it from shedding just its light
and your fingers —you write
as if this stone was already black

and step by step your child-like name
pinned on to become its last breath
while you steer the lettering back home

leave spaces for this iron waterfall
to point from under some mountainside
at whispers that no longer move

smothered by braids, shoulders, kisses
that are yours, oceans, winds, mornings
blacker than this dirt and lost.

*

This stone on your forehead
stays white between these hands
that never let go though you

were not thinking about winter
and distances filled with peaks
that cannot be saved by groans

and thinning trees now that rain
seeps into your ears and shadows
flow past one by one, held down

by a stone that blankets the Earth
—you hear nothing about these kisses
turning into snow and moonlight

as something invisible :plumes
slowly covering you from behind
with emptiness and bare shoulders.

*

Even if these waves are calmed
this rock deserves respect
though there's no grave

not yet that first turn
to the side, smoothed
the way all night your eyes

stare at the beach, guiding it
to where it was born
already head down, embraced

—this rock is lost, blind
filled with the light
that still cools the sun

takes on its great weight
then pours back the sand
only stone can hear

forget it once was human
and in your arms
would become frail, shatter

just for the name inside
dropping to the bottom
that wants to let go.

*

With a sudden glow one leg
begins to bend though your heart
creaks, each step growing sunlight

from rocks the way mountains
flower just by breaking apart
though inside nothing moves
waits to brush against these dead
—they know what happened
write down the place, have the lock

and you walk by as the same few days
or weeks or now and then
a put-aside, half shows up

just for the view, slowly, as if you
are no longer alive, left as you were
face to face for a long time.

*

Windswept, this radio
broken open with its stations
one on top each other

though what you hear
is its dust, bleeding
the way this rag, half doll

half straw, half dirt
scraping till a darkness
oozes from your fingertips

bent over, garbled
—she couldn't tell it's you
from far away, listening for her.

*

As if a rope, half bone
half pulled from your chest
the way this dead branch

tells you everything then closes
though the wood won't burn
  —so many things are made from doorways

and she was left inside
with nothing to sit on or a stone
that will fall by itself, broken off

to die alone, whispering goodbye
for two and this dirt not yet
just another hole that weighs too much.

*

This battered window box
has found an opening
—with a single flower

is taking on the sun
though you use well water
fitting it into its shadow

as if madness needs a corner
for its darkness reaching out
the way your heart was filled

with river noise
that has nothing left to give
—what you hear is the sun

swallowing ice as the antidote
to flower after flower and the mist
from someone breathing.

*

You were buried in the afternoon
and yet the moon was lost
on its way to the sea —what's left

is each night step by step
swallowing the light it needs
to swell —your grave will brighten soon

grow branches, more names, splash
—here is that sea and from the night
a grief-stone no bigger than a star

will fall into the waves rising as sunlight
made from sunlight and whitecaps
that pass by as spray that is not shoreline

right and left, smelling from salt
and your shadow with nothing left to let go
shimmering as if something happened.

*

It was a needless rinse, this bowl
half wood, half smelling from wood
that's been taken away, trembling

as if today will be its last
though you gather up the spoon
holding it close and your arm

keeps it warm, covered with a stream
beginning to root as the emptiness
you lift to your lips without trying.

*

It's not a map yet there's hope
—you unfold old times
as if one morning in February

you would spread your arms
and land became land again
stayed behind as the snow

still tying down the Earth
—a small envelope, kept empty
the way you would reach for her hand

and inside the air was warm
though there's no rain, no grass
not yet a place for a name.

*

It's what you do, the mirror
becomes a sheet, the bed
is in there somewhere —you squint

and under this frost the glass
is warmed, covers your eyes
even more than tomorrow

—you end each day inside a hill
on its way to this sink
where without any hope the faucet

holds your hand and all the time
pulls the mist back in
as skies and kisses clouding over

flowing into an empty dress
worn only at night
lets you breathe again

—without a blanket, without a pillow
you barely see the silence
covering a mouth with your lips.

*

You learn to hammer in the dark
though no one studies the hillside
how it still leans across your arms

the way creeks cast for weeds
and edges —so little is known
why iron takes root in your gut

and the same rain
drags from these wooden shingles
the constant tilt still trying to make it down

—you seal this hole by weeping into it
with a nail that's bent, struggling
to talk, to find its way and the sea.

*

As if these gravestones were once a forest
between each there's still the breeze
from wood and leaves and winter

though under your fingertips the initials
warm, are already stretching out
the way a beginner tree wants to be lit

then at its highest even in the cold
grows a small stone that will ripen
and stay red for the arrow

carved around two rivers and the heart
brought closer, smelling from the caress
that is not a blouse or its ashes.

*

What was siphoned off the sun
could just as easily be this tree
and each branch carried out

struggling with moss and faraway
—who can tell it's not this tree's
last chance to sort the light

as if going somewhere was still possible
that love too is possible —all this wood
even in winter arriving to gather you up

as leaves, shining, smelling from dew
already beginning to blossom, impatient
for arms and shoulders and the fire.

*

And stubborn yet these wicks
warm the light they need
to blossom as stone

then cling, smell from hair
burning inside, clawing for roots
heated by butterflies

and the afternoons coming together
to light the fire, be a noon
where there was none before.

*

You never get used to it
left and right —moonlight
all that's left on your grave

each night heavier, bitter
with no place to fall
sometimes as snow, sometimes

counting on pebbles from others
all night bringing stars
to strike the ground over and over

covering you with shadows
and still you're cold
come here as paths and distances.

*

When you come, come singing
not with words :hum
is what changes a heart into wings

the way echoes stay in the sky
as the long journey home
for butterflies and leaves —come

with trees, then sap rising
till its roots make a noise
that will never tire, wants

to be a river but come by air
bring bells that flow, bring branches
feathers, bring a bag that's empty.

*

What's left is its wingtip
though you can still tell time
by pointing end over end

the way lovers come to this park
take that last look back
burning alive in each other's arms

—the plane never had a chance
and you're not supposed to wave like that
making room for its enormous death

though every night begins as soot
from benches, thighs, kisses, the on and on
thrown in the fire for later.

*

You draw a star on the calendar
and without touching your lips
an unexpected breeze reminds you

there's now in writing where light
will slow down and the days take forever
to remember someone is holding your hand

embracing August the way a rock still alive
is broken in half and without a sound
added to the fire —it's a see-through star

and under your fingers forgets
it has a shadow just now starting out
will cover the Earth with a night

that goes on burning —you use a pencil
for its wood that knows nothing but corners
kept sharp even when turning to stone.

*

What did you expect! with just its scent
an old love note lights this lamp
the way bats sip from flowers and darkness

and though the ink has soured
it's the night that's draining you
as the arm around her shoulders

—word by word it becomes again
a butterfly, is dipping into the flourish
over your name lit by hers and shining.

*

You weakened the paint with salt
from the off-white evenings
changing colors in the open

misled the can by lifting it
close to your arms then campfires
and songs still getting together

reaching out for the trails
that dip into your heart
are carried along as the streams

wanting to rush through walls
one by one —you begin
with your fingers, disguised

as there and back and thirst
then mostly it's the photographs
and certificates whose frames

were already promised
spiders, moths, corners
that have no other place to hide.

*

You walk clinging to streams
from when the Earth was shattered
still gathers up the rocks broken off

for light where a sky should be
help the lost find their way home
and though her grave was left behind

you come here to start a fire by naming it
slowly after the tree that widened, became a sea
and every night washes over this stone

guiding it back as a singing —each leaf
already the warm breeze that reaches up
no longer smoke from arms and distances.

*

Everything on this wall clouds over
at first, a window then opens
swallowing the sky mid-air

though here you are, hammering
—this picture frame was already too heavy
is pressing against the glass

as the unbearable sorrow when its likeness
can only be found in wood
where you no longer hear your fingers tighten

from soaking in the sweat that clings to a nail
bent and bleeding then hidden in back, holds on
to what it remembers falling from the sky

as one after another, yet there it is
in drops —don't you hear them telling you
to step back from her photograph.

*

Plane after plane till all the pieces
arrive as flowers —it's winter
returning now to nest and every morning

begins with an ancient chill
unfolding over and over for lift
and mountains though you take hold

try to escape its turbulence
—against all odds you become a breeze
are losing altitude, your voice slows

then stalls, spins and the scent
falls against your chest as snow
that stays in one place and waits.

*

Drop by drop, its silence
holds on to the mud and each other
though this puddle sparkles

from tides that are not sunlight
—what you hear are the shells
darkening and their nest

breaking open for more air
the way you toss in a pebble
just to hear its ripples

as the splash from your first day
still reaching for shore, lower, lower
and flight no longer possible.

*

Side by side a planet that has no star
you wander for years
which means remorse has taken hold

the way this dried love note
never lets go its warmth
though the afternoon becomes a place

for constellations, is wobbling
as silence and the end
—where else can it hide

is more forgiving than a period
left where a well-meaning sentence
gave all it had and for the first time

a darkness was falling from above
bird-like, spreading out as far away
around and around, over and over again.

*

The rock that sparked a supernova
circles this lamp no longer moving
stays dark though every star

is hunted down by a crack in the wall
or someone else's window till one by one
they become a reef that smells from salt

—every headstone here is lit
with a smaller stone set off at night
with a boatman as dew and losing itself.

*

A few hours and all the stars
come together where the sun
waits in one piece again —to survive

you wear a bracelet in bed
let the beads circle down
as if in the dark the window

becomes a mirror, could be rain
pressed against the glass
where some sea is drifting as small holes

being filled with falling tides
and the madness not yet a morning
though glow is everything

when surrounded by a shadow
no longer feeling its way across this wall
to escape the corners already afternoons.

*

You fill in the name then prop it
with the same black ink
that will widen for the underline

and keep the word from falling
as your shadow still holding on
to the pen and your fingertips

that stop by twice a day
and each evening draw a name
on wood the way rings in a tree

keep count how many times
you circle her graveside
to keep it from moving, warmed

under a sun made from paper
whose silence goes on living
as just another word for two.

*

Although you wait for midnight
a last minute breeze is scattering this dust
with enchantment —the rag

already the dress Cinderella will wear
and this neglected window pane
the slipper left behind as the charm

from some invisible sea where the rush
fills with sunlight —wave over wave
becomes the Ferris-wheels

coiling the way all night the carriage
is kept warm by stars allowed in
till once upon a time comes back

as shattered glass and ice
where the window opens
only for its darkness and the cold.

www.ingramcontent.com/pod-product-compliance
Lightning Source LLC
LaVergne TN
LVHW041629070426
835507LV00008B/525